CAREERS IN COMPUTER TECHNOLOGY™

CAREERS IN

Computer
Support

JERI FREEDMAN

ROSEN
PUBLISHING

Published in 2014 by The Rosen Publishing Group, Inc.
29 East 21st Street, New York, NY 10010

Library of Congress Cataloging-in-Publication Data

Freedman, Jeri.
Careers in computer support/Jeri Freedman.—1st ed.—
New York: Rosen, © 2014
     p. cm.—(Careers in computer technology)
Includes bibliographical references and index.
ISBN 978-1-4488-9594-6
1. Computer science—Vocational guidance—Juvenile literature.
2. Computer service industry—Vocational guidance—Juvenile literature.
I. Title.
QA76.25 .F74 2014
004.023

Manufactured in the United States of America

CPSIA Compliance Information: Batch #S13YA: For further information, contact Rosen Publishing, New York, New York, at
1-800-237-9932.

Contents

Computers are everywhere in life today. People use desktop computers in offices and computerized equipment on the job. They use personal computers at home to entertain themselves, stay in touch with friends and family, find information, and shop. Mobile technology has resulted in tiny computers in the form of smartphones and convenient-to-carry tablets. All of this technology has created a tremendous need for computer support. The demand for individuals with expertise in computer support is greater than ever before. And this demand is expected only to increase in the coming decades. Therefore, the field of computer support is likely to provide a secure career, even in times when the economy is struggling.

Careers exist in computer support at all levels, from entry-level hardware technicians to network administrators, information technology managers, and at the highest executive level, chief technology officers. Computer support staff can work in large corporations, nonprofit organizations, small companies, retail stores, and computer services companies. Computer support professionals may work with computer hardware, software, or both. They may work directly with the public or work behind the scenes to keep a company's systems running. This variety of options means that support personnel can choose an environment that suits their interests and personality.

Computer support careers can be demanding, requiring long hours and attention to detail. Because computer technology and software change constantly, computer professionals must keep updating their skills.

Application support engineers run maintenance operations at a company that provides television services for mobile devices. The growth in mobile devices has created many new computer support jobs.

In addition, work hours can be long and irregular, and many projects have strict deadlines. Computer support professionals must deal tactfully with users in stressful situations. However, there are many advantages to this career. In the computer field, exciting technological changes are constantly taking place. Pay is usually good because of the technical expertise required. Also, jobs in computer support often have a strong career path. Professionals can move to higher levels of responsibility with larger salaries as they gain more experience.

A variety of jobs in computer support are explored here. Information is provided on the education and training needed to qualify for these jobs. In addition, practical advice is provided on how to get a first computer support job.

CHAPTER 1

The Computer Support Industry

Computer support professionals work in many different kinds of companies and organizations. They also work with a variety of computer hardware, software, and systems. The following are some of the environments and industries in which computer support staff commonly work.

JOBS IN INDUSTRY

Computers are used heavily in business today. Businesses use databases to store data about customers and keep track of sales and marketing information. Databases are collections of electronic records that contain important business data, for example, details about customers or orders. Businesses also use management information systems to analyze information on the company's products, competitors, and activities in order to make good business decisions. For example, a company might analyze data about potential customers to target those most likely to buy the company's products. Or, it might analyze the results of its advertising campaigns.

Businesses use financial computer systems to do bookkeeping and keep track of investments. Marketing and advertising personnel use computer graphics systems to design brochures and other marketing materials. Web sites provide information on the company and its products to members of the public.

Stock traders rely on computers to perform their jobs. Processing client orders quickly is critical for a stock brokerage. In many companies, keeping computers operating is vital for business operations.

One of the most important types of computerized system today is the security system. Concerns about crime and terrorism have increased the use of integrated security systems. An integrated system includes security cameras, keycard locks, and other security devices. Computers control and monitor access and record information about who uses various areas and resources. Some security systems include special computer programs, such as facial recognition software, to help security personnel keep out unauthorized people.

Many companies manufacture products. Today, manufacturing processes are often automated and controlled by computer systems. Even when employees operate machinery, many machines include computers that help them run.

The assembly line is not the only place where computers are used in industry. Many manufacturers use computer systems to keep track of their inventory of both parts and finished goods. Inventory management systems track how many of each part are available and alert managers when parts are running low. Sometimes such systems automatically order parts when the amount on hand reaches a certain level. They also keep track of parts received. Purchasing systems keep track of orders and are used to match received goods to purchase orders. Sales systems help keep track of product orders and shipping information.

Utilities use computers to operate power plants and to control the distribution of power throughout the electrical grid.

All of these computer systems must be networked, maintained, updated, and fixed when they are not working properly. People who use the computers must be trained and helped when they have problems.

JOBS IN NONPROFITS, HEALTH CARE, AND EDUCATION

Computers play a large part in charities, health care, and education today. Charities use computer systems to manage their fund-raising efforts. Such systems use special software that records and tracks donations and donors. They also use computers for office work and bookkeeping and for the creation of fund-raising and presentation materials. If a charity runs special projects, it may also use project management software to keep track of them.

JOB-RELATED STATISTICS: COMPUTER SUPPORT

The U.S. Bureau of Labor Statistics (BLS) estimates that in 2010 there were over six hundred thousand jobs for computer support specialists. The BLS expects that number to grow at the rate of 18 percent annually. The demand for network and computer systems administrators is expected to grow even faster, at 28 percent per year, and the demand for database administrators is expected to grow at a rate of 31 percent per year. One of the advantages of looking for a job in this field is that opportunities exist at a variety of levels and in a vast range of companies, industries, and organizations.

All types of educational institutions use computer systems. Colleges and universities often have several different computer networks. For example, they may have one network for normal business functions, such as finance and office work, and a second for the use by those engaged in scientific and other research. Colleges and universities often have computer labs for student use as well. Computer networks in higher education are often massive, covering numerous buildings across an entire campus. If a university has multiple locations, the computer network may cover a city or region. Computer systems in education may be used for tracking student information and grades, creating brochures and catalogs, fund-raising, research, library cataloging, and security, among other functions. Colleges and universities are more likely than other organizations to require a college degree for employment.

An information technology support specialist shows a nurse how to use a handheld device to access patient records. Training personnel in how to use new devices is one support responsibility.

In hospitals, medical clinics, and doctors' offices, computers have long been used to keep track of patient records and for billing. Recent laws passed under President Barack Obama's administration have expanded the use of computers in health care. These laws require health care providers to use centralized medical systems to keep track of patients' medical information, including symptoms, test results, prescriptions, and the like. The goal of keeping all the patient's information on a centralized computer is to allow medical professionals in different departments and facilities to access it. This approach is designed to reduce duplication of tests, as well as to cut down on errors.

GOVERNMENT COMPUTER SUPPORT JOBS

Local, state, and federal governments use computers for a variety of purposes, including business operations such as finance and budgeting. Government agencies and departments, such as state and federal environmental protection agencies, NASA, and the Department of Energy, use computer systems for scientific analysis and research.

The military uses computer systems for both routine business and special purposes. Computers are used to organize

The Texas National Guard uses computer-controlled cameras to monitor the U.S.-Mexico border at the Border Control Processing Center in El Paso, Texas. Computer support is important for national security systems.

and control the distribution of personnel and matériel, analyze intelligence information, and plan military operations. Computers are also used in communication systems and in engineering applications. In the field, military personnel use computers to operate drones and in advanced weapon systems such as missile guidance systems.

Local, state, and federal law enforcement agencies use computer systems to access information on known and suspected terrorists and criminals and to analyze evidence. Federal agencies, such as the Department of Homeland Security, Central Intelligence Agency, and National Security Agency, use computers to acquire and analyze information about potential threats to the United States.

COMPUTER SERVICES COMPANIES

There are many different industries in which one can work in computer support. Some people work for companies that provide computer support services to other companies, businesses, or individuals. Computer services companies range from one-person operations to large chains. Some operate as small stores or independent contractors who provide support directly to individual consumers. These businesses set up computers, create home networks, and provide troubleshooting when users need help. Often these operations provide both walk-in and in-home assistance.

Small business owners and freelancers (individuals who provide services directly to clients) may make a significant amount of money because computer services are in high demand, and they can charge sizable fees for their expertise.

An example of a computer services operation is the Geek Squad from electronics retailer Best Buy. Support staff repair customers' computers and other devices and help with setup, virus protection, data backup, and the like.

However, they must pay for their own benefits, such as health insurance, and cover the costs associated with running a business, such as rent, utilities, and advertising. Also, depending on the services they offer, they may have to respond to problems at all hours and any day of the week. If they work alone, they must do all the work themselves, which can be stressful. Small business owners who have employees must make enough money to cover their salaries and benefits as well. Those thinking of operating their own business should be knowledgeable about basic business subjects such as finance, bookkeeping, budgeting, marketing, and management, in addition to having knowledge of computer hardware and software.

Computer support services are also provided at in-house service departments in retail stores, such as Best Buy. Computer support staff who work in these service centers perform the same tasks as their independent counterparts. Employees who work for retail stores and small computer services businesses receive a salary and, often, benefits. They have the security of a regular income and benefits, and they do not have the overhead associated with running their own business. However, they may not earn as much as independent contractors.

Some computer services companies focus on providing support to businesses. Many of their clients are small- to medium-sized businesses that are not large enough to have their own information technology department. These computer services companies assist businesses in designing their computer networks and purchasing computers. They install computers on companies' premises, install and update computer software, and fix hardware and software problems for companies.

Such services companies may work on an as-needed basis: companies will call them when they need help with specific computer-related issues. Often, however, the service company will have a contract with a business. In this case, the business pays a monthly or annual fee to the computer services company, and the services company provides help whenever it is needed. In such cases, computer professionals receive calls from the client when there is a problem and either resolve it over the phone or travel to the client's location to fix it. Employees of companies that provide services to businesses often must take turns being on call. This means that, if a client has a computer problem outside of normal business hours, that person must respond and deal with the problem.

Working for a computer services company requires excellent people skills as well as technical knowledge. One may have to explain complex technological topics to people with little or no technical knowledge. Patience and tact are required to deal with customers who are stressed out because their computer system is not functioning properly.

CHAPTER 2

Types of Computer Support

There are different types of computer support one can choose as a career. Which path is most appropriate for an individual depends on one's skills, interests, and personality. Some people are more comfortable in small, informal companies, where they can be more independent and have more flexibility. Some prefer large corporations, which have more bureaucracy but offer better pay and more opportunity for advancement. Other people prefer to be their own boss. While some people enjoy working with physical devices, others prefer to work with software and applications. Some would rather fix things and not have to deal with the public, whereas others like to work with and help people. We will explore all of these aspects of computer support.

HARDWARE

The physical parts that make up computer systems are called hardware. Computer hardware requires support, repair, and maintenance to keep it running. A computer system consists of the following components:

- A central processing unit (CPU). This is the main part of the computer that processes information.
- A monitor on which to view the output of the computer's operations.

- User input devices, such as a mouse or trackball and keyboard.
- A place to store data, such as a hard drive or flash drive.

In addition to taking care of computers and their parts, computer support staff must be familiar with a range of peripherals used with computers. Peripherals are devices that provide additional functionality when attached to a computer. The most common peripheral is a printer. Other peripherals include Web cameras (Webcams), speakers, and drawing tablets. Hardware support might require assembling computers from components, testing components to make sure they work or to identify problems, and replacing nonworking components. It might also involve upgrading computers by adding new internal components or replacing old components with newer versions.

Many types of hardware components require software to provide them with instructions on how to run. This software is called a driver. Computer support professionals must install drivers. They must also configure a computer's operating system software to use a particular model of software or peripheral.

In addition to servicing desktop personal computers (PCs), today's computer support professionals often assist users with mobile computers, such as notebooks, tablets, and smartphones.

At one time, businesses ran their computing processes off one large computer, called a mainframe. Today, however, companies usually provide their employees with individual PCs. These computers are connected to a larger-capacity PC, called a server. The individual computers can download data

Computer hardware and software change constantly as companies like Microsoft Corporation develop new operating systems, such as Windows 8, and new devices, such as tablets.

and documents from the server and upload data and documents back to the server for storage. This connected system of computers is called a network. In addition, a network often includes peripherals such as printers, which are shared by users. Computer networks require special security hardware and software to control access to the system. Computer support personnel are responsible for keeping the network secure and running properly by installing, monitoring, and updating this hardware and software.

SOFTWARE

In order for computers to perform functions, they require software programs. Some software programs, known as

PROS AND CONS OF COMPUTER SUPPORT CAREERS

Because they require a lot of technical skill and training, computer support jobs are often highly paid. When the economy is slow, finding a job in the field is easier than in many industries simply because of the large number of computers and computer systems in use. In addition, in organizations that have information technology departments, there are often opportunities for promotion as one gains more skills and experience. There is great job security in the field because of the ever-increasing need for those with technical know-how.

The major downside to a computer support career is stress. Personnel often work under time pressure, dealing with managers, employees, or users who are having computer problems while working under deadline. There is a high likelihood of being faced with many different users and tasks, all of which need to be addressed in a timely fashion. Support staff may also have to respond to problems outside of normal business hours. In addition, there may be budget limitations that affect staff's ability to obtain needed equipment and software, which can be frustrating.

Computer support staff must stay up-to-date on the latest hardware and software and stay current with the available patches and fixes for problems as they are identified. Computer support is a field that can be demanding, but it provides high pay and good advancement opportunities.

applications, are used to perform specific tasks. Examples of applications are the Microsoft Word word-processing program and Adobe Photoshop photo-editing software.

An important aspect of computer support is installing, maintaining, and troubleshooting software programs. Computer support staff are responsible for making sure that companies have the proper licenses for the software they use, upgrading the software so it has the latest features, and applying patches to the software when necessary. Patches are software updates issued by the software manufacturer that fix problems with the software. Computer support staff often help users troubleshoot issues with applications as well.

WEB SITE SUPPORT

It is common today for a company—large or small—to have a Web site on the Internet. Such Web sites have become a major way for potential customers to learn about a company's products, services, and activities. In the case of retail businesses, the company may allow customers to buy products directly from the Web site.

In addition to a public Web site, many companies also have an internal Web site for their employees, called an intranet. This type of site is used to inform employees about policies and company activities. Sometimes, it also allows employees to share information with each other.

Companies use a third type of Web site to connect with their suppliers. This type of Web site might, for example, allow suppliers of parts to log in to the company's inventory system and check whether stocks of parts need to be replenished. All of these kinds of Web sites must be kept up and running and modified when necessary. This work is called Web site support.

USER SUPPORT

Whereas some types of computer support take place largely behind the scenes, user support involves working directly with people who have computer problems. User support includes teaching users how to use computers, related devices, and peripherals. It also involves fixing problems for users. Typical user support tasks include showing a user how to access features in an application, setting up an employee's notebook or tablet to access the company's computer network, or setting up an employee's smartphone.

User support personnel may also work for a computer hardware or software manufacturer. In this case, they may be responsible for helping users set up the company's products or solve problems that arise with the products. This may be done over the phone or online. Sometimes it involves remotely accessing the user's computer via special software that can be downloaded to it.

CHAPTER ③
Computer Support Jobs

Because there are so many types of computer support jobs, their responsibilities, projects, and tasks vary. The following sections discuss several types of jobs in computer support and the particular tasks and activities performed in them.

COMPUTER TECHNICIAN

Computer technicians fix computers and sometimes install and set up software on the machines. They must be familiar with the various hardware components inside computers and understand how they are installed and connected. Computer technicians run tests on computers that are not operating correctly to identify the source of problems. They then replace or fix malfunctioning parts. Common tasks include taking a user's files off of an old computer and installing them on a new one or installing a new operating system (such as a new version of Windows) on an existing computer. Computer technicians may work in the information technology department at a company or organization. Alternately, they may be employed in a retail setting, where they set up and fix computers for customers.

SYSTEMS AND NETWORK ADMINISTRATORS

Systems administrators and network administrators maintain, upgrade, secure, and fix the computer systems and networks used in businesses and organizations. A computer network is a group of computers connected to each other through a central computer, called a server. The networked computers use the server to exchange electronic files. Most computers in work-places today are connected with cables and other hardware. Sometimes employees also connect to networks wirelessly via notebook or tablet computers or even smartphones. Special software installed on the server, called network-operating soft-ware, controls the network.

Systems or network administrators manage the physi-cal aspects of the network, such as adding more devices as needed. They also monitor the network to make sure that users can upload, download, and process information without long waits or other problems. Systems or network administra-tors upgrade the software and hardware and fix any problems that arise with an upgrade. They also secure the network, keeping unauthorized people from accessing the computers or the software that runs on them. Administrators in this posi-tion also make sure that the data on the computer network is backed up and stored in a safe location so that it can be restored in the event of disaster.

Being a systems or network administrator requires a knowledge of both computer hardware and software. Most

Testing, installing, and updating the components of a company's network are key responsibilities of network administrators. They must know how to configure components from different manufacturers.

professionals acquire this knowledge through formal education. In addition, they often gain professional certifications from manufacturers of computer and networking software and hardware, such as Microsoft and Cisco Systems. These certifications demonstrate to prospective employers that one has the required degree of skill in using particular technologies. Acquiring a professional certification requires studying material supplied by the company and passing a test.

DATABASE ADMINISTRATOR

Databases are collections of records that contain information. Companies use databases for many purposes. Accounting uses them to keep track of customer and vendor information. Human resources uses them to keep track of employee information. Marketing uses databases to keep track of customer and product information. Research and development uses them to keep track of test results. The purchasing department uses them to keep track of inventory and order information. And nonprofits use them to keep track of donor information.

The information in databases is stored in the form of electronic records. Database software allows these records to be sorted and analyzed according to specific pieces of data contained in them. For instance, employees might be sorted according to department, salary, or position. Customers might be sorted by city, state, or region, or the size of orders over the past year. Databases are often created using database software from companies such as Oracle Corporation. Database software uses a special programming language—typically, structured query language (SQL)—to retrieve information.

The person responsible for maintaining the databases and assisting users is called a database administrator. Database administrators are responsible for the maintenance, upgrading, and security of an organization's databases. They are also expected to fix problems with the databases. Database administrators must have a strong knowledge of database software. They must be able to interact with company employees to

A wide variety of organizations require database administrators. For instance, this database is used to keep track of information on wildlife. Thus, database administrators can work in almost any area of interest.

help them find the information they need to do their jobs. They also help employees deal with any problems they may encounter while using the database.

Database administrators are responsible for keeping the data in the databases safe. They establish security procedures to keep unauthorized users from accessing the data. They also back up the database so that the information can be restored if there is a computer failure or a disaster at the facility. Database administrators use software to monitor the performance of the database. If users experience long wait times when trying to access data, the database administrator has to figure out why this is occurring and fix the problem.

IT MANAGEMENT

Many companies and organizations have information technology (IT) departments, which are devoted to handling their computer needs. Such departments consist of anything from a few to dozens of computer professionals who are responsible for specific aspects of the organization's computer systems. The head of such a department is the IT manager. The manager does not usually handle the hands-on support tasks, especially in larger departments. Instead, the IT manager oversees the department, hiring and supervising the staff and organizing the functions within the department.

Information technology managers are responsible for running the IT department, supervising the IT staff, training them, and assisting them in solving problems when they arise.

The IT manager approves the decisions of the employees he or she supervises, including their requests to purchase software and equipment. He or she may also meet with senior management to make recommendations for meeting the company's needs for technology resources and to obtain approval for large purchases. The IT manager is responsible for creating the departmental budget and for tracking expenditures to make sure they don't exceed those in the budget.

An IT manager needs training and experience in computer technology. However, because this is a managerial position, additional training or education in business skills is often helpful for success. Therefore, those interested in moving into management typically take some business and management courses.

Computer support is a critical function in most companies. Large companies often have higher levels of IT management beyond the IT manager, such as director of information technology, and even chief information officer (CIO). Chief information officer is a senior management position. The CIO is responsible for high-level planning and for overseeing all of the company's computer operations.

HELP DESK JOBS

"Help desk" is the name given to the business department that answers users' computer-related questions and helps them solve computer problems. Some help desk personnel may work with internal users at a company. Others may work for a manufacturer of computer hardware or software, helping its customers. Individual consumers or employees of

Help desk staff must have good people skills as well as technical knowledge. They must guide nervous users through the steps necessary to resolve their hardware or software problems.

companies using the manufacturer's products call the help desk for support. Help desk staff answer users' questions and walk them through procedures to identify what is causing the problem. Sometimes they download remote-access software onto users' computers. This software allows the help desk personnel to take control of a user's computer from a distance in order to identify or fix problems.

INTERVIEW WITH A DIRECTOR OF TECHNICAL OPERATIONS

Miles Freedman is the director of technical operations at a software-as-a-service (SaaS) company. His company maintains databases of information for companies that purchase its services, collecting and analyzing sales information to help them identify sales opportunities.

WHAT DO YOU DO IN YOUR JOB?

I manage five departments at a company providing sales analytics data to Fortune 500 companies. I do the following:

- Manage the software on the Web site, which is called platform operations
- Support the platform internally (ensure the system keeps running for maximum availability, and fix things when they go wrong)
- Provide customer support
- Implement security
- Do database administration

WHAT DO YOU LIKE ABOUT YOUR JOB?

It allows me to work in a fast-paced environment with many very intelligent people who keep me challenged on a daily basis.

WHAT DO YOU DISLIKE ABOUT YOUR JOB?

Sometimes very intelligent people want a bit too much input into the way things are done, down to the nuts-and-bolts level.

WHAT EDUCATION AND SKILLS ARE NEEDED TO DO THE JOB?

A bachelor of science (BS) degree in a computer science or engineering program or relevant experience.

WHAT ADVICE WOULD YOU OFFER A YOUNG PERSON CONSIDERING THIS CAREER?

Go to college! And get a degree in a hard subject: math, science, or business. Getting the first job is the toughest, and having the right kind of college degree is crucial. Later on in your career it matters less, and your experience is what companies look at.

WHEN YOU HIRE SOMEONE FOR A POSITION IN COMPUTER SUPPORT, WHAT DO YOU LOOK FOR?

I look for hard skills like knowledge of certain technologies (hardware support, Microsoft Outlook and Office knowledge, SQL skills) that meet the company's needs. But I also look closely at soft skills: project management, general personality, people skills, and problem-solving ability. Often those skills are overlooked, and they can be the most important in the ability to execute in a support role. Honing those skills and selling them at an interview is just as critical as your knowledge of specific computer or software technologies.

PROFESSIONALISM IN THE WORKPLACE

Many computer support staff members see themselves as working with machines, not people. However, in the workplace, it is always important to present yourself professionally. Some computer professionals work primarily behind the scenes and have little contact with the public or customers. In this case, neat and clean slacks and a shirt or sweater may be appropriate dress. If support staff deal with a company's management, customers, or clients, then a shirt and tie for males and a pantsuit, business-appropriate dress, or skirt and blouse for females is proper attire. Management is more likely to respect and promote employees who project a professional image. Management wants people with good technical skills but also values those who can represent the company well.

Small companies, especially those that employ only a few people, are often flexible about their employees' work attire and accept casual dress. However, when customers, clients, or outside professionals, such as potential investors, are likely to be present, employees are expected to dress well in order to help the firm make a professional impression.

Computer support professionals often interact with users inside and outside their company. They represent the company to external users. Therefore, they need to behave professionally with everyone they meet on the job. They should show up on time to appointments, return phone calls, and behave honestly and responsibly on the job. First and foremost, being professional means always doing the best work one is capable of doing.

CAREER PATHS

There are a lot of advancement opportunities in the field of computer support. Very often people start by working in an entry-level position in the field, such as computer support technician. If an employee is in a medium-to-large company with a multiperson IT department, he or she may be able to advance within the company. Otherwise, after gaining experience, a computer support professional may choose to move on to a higher-level position in another company.

In a corporate environment, one can advance to a network or systems administrator position and then to an IT manager, director of IT, vice president of IT, and even to a chief information officer (CIO) position. In retail operations, one can move from computer technician or customer support representative to manager. One then might move to more senior positions with responsibilities for supervising staff at multiple branches of the retail operation. Advancement in the computer field often requires continual updating of one's knowledge by taking courses or certifications, in addition to performing well in one's current job.

CHAPTER 4

Preparing for a Career in Computer Support

Computer support requires technical knowledge. This knowledge may be gained through formal education that leads to a degree; practical, hands-on training; or a combination of these. A large number of technical schools, colleges, and universities offer programs in computer science. Colleges and universities offer two-year associate's degrees, four-year bachelor's degrees, and advanced degrees. Technical schools offer associate's degree and bachelor's degree programs. Some vocational high schools also offer training in computer science as a career.

Preparation for a career in computer support begins well before college. In order to ensure success in college, it is necessary to acquire a solid grounding in basic skills in high school.

HIGH SCHOOL

Many high schools offer courses in computers, and it is a good idea to take them. In addition to providing students with basic computing skills, taking an introductory course is a good way for teens to find out if computers really interest them.

Working with computers requires a solid knowledge of math and science. College-level computer science and information technology programs contain a large number of math and science courses. Therefore, the more basic math and science knowledge students gain in high school, the easier they will find it to succeed in computer science in college.

Students should take courses in algebra and precalculus, as well as calculus if it is offered. Advanced math, such as

High school students work with calculators and computers in math class. Because computer technology relies heavily on mathematics, the more math students study in school, the better.

calculus, is the basis for computer algorithms (sets of steps for performing tasks). Statistics is another area of math that is important to understand. Not all high schools offer courses in statistics, but if it is possible to take one, by all means do so. Statistics are used in the analysis of computer performance and in database administration. It is also important to study physics. Physics helps explain the basic scientific principles that underlie electronics. Studying these principles allows students to understand how and why computer hardware operates the way it does—and why it sometimes malfunctions.

In school, and someday in a job, some of the most important skills are obtained through hands-on experience.

Therefore, if your school has a computer club that offers experience in practical computer skills, join it if you are serious about a computer career. If the school has a computer lab, volunteer to help out in it. This is a good way to learn how to work with computers firsthand. It also provides experience one can include in a résumé when later applying for a job.

Computer skills are not the only skills needed to be successful in this field. Succeeding in a computer technology career in the real world requires a variety of nontechnical skills. The time to begin learning those skills is in high school.

Among the most critical are good communication skills. The ability to organize ideas and present them clearly, in both verbal and written form, is of great importance. Few careers involve as much interaction with other people as computer support. People in the field must be able to extract information from flustered users and, in turn, explain problems, solutions, and technical information in a way that nontechnical people can understand. Except for freelance computer consultants, most computer support personnel work in departments with others. Therefore, they must be able to communicate effectively with coworkers and management as well as with users. They must be able to clearly communicate information and ideas both verbally and in written reports. As a result, knowledge of English grammar is very important. If your school offers a public speaking course, it may be useful to take it. Such a course gives students experience speaking in public and teaches them how to communicate clearly when speaking to individuals or groups.

Definitely take a typing course if your school offers it. Working with computers requires a great deal of typing. Learning to type properly can save a lot of time. Approach all your work in high school with attention to detail and the goal of getting assignments done on time. Developing these habits while in school will serve you well when working in the computer support field.

HIGHER EDUCATION

Students can learn computing and programming skills in a variety of ways. Courses are available in particular aspects of hardware and software, and there are books and CDs that offer training in specific technologies. Some people simply learn on the job, often while employed at a small company. However, the most efficient and effective way to prepare for a career in computer support is to get a college degree in computer science or information technology.

Higher education provides thorough and systematic training in current technologies and techniques. This knowledge equips students for what they are likely to encounter in the workplace. College-level education also provides students with knowledge of the science behind the technology. This knowledge can later be applied to understand how new technologies work as they emerge in the marketplace.

A college education also teaches students how to analyze information and solve problems, which are valuable skills on the job. Completing a degree demonstrates to employers that a potential employee has the basic skills they require. This is especially important for candidates who have little practical experience to offer. Beyond this, it also demonstrates that a person can follow through and reach a goal successfully. Finally, having a college degree can make it easier to obtain a promotion to higher levels in IT.

College courses in computer technology provide a systematic way to learn how computers are engineered.

Many colleges offer four-year bachelor's degree programs in their computer science departments as well as master's degree and Ph.D. programs. Some schools also offer two-year associate's degrees. Technical institutes offer both four-year degree programs and two-year associate's degree programs. Some community colleges offer associate's degree programs as well; these can be a cost-effective alternative to a four-year program. Associate's degree programs concentrate on particular technical skills, such as computer network administration. They are designed to prepare students for entry-level positions working with computer hardware and software. Often it is possible to transfer credits obtained in an associate's degree program to another college or university and pursue a four-year bachelor's degree.

Many medium-sized and large companies offer tuition reimbursement programs. Such programs reimburse employees for the cost of additional education that they can apply in their jobs. Thus, one option for those who can't afford a four-year college program is to obtain basic training at a technical school or community college and pursue further education part-time while working. Many technical schools and colleges offer part-time and evening programs in computer science.

In addition to degrees, many institutions offer certificate programs in specific areas of computer science. These programs focus on a particular skill or technology and award a certificate to those who complete the program successfully. The certificate specifies that the individual has mastered that technology. Certificate programs range from a few months to a year or two in length. They are especially useful for people working in the field who need to learn new technologies as they come along. For example, someone might want to pursue a certificate program to learn the latest techniques in cybersecurity.

College programs generally cover a variety of aspects of computer hardware and software, rather than focusing specifically on computer support. A college student should take a general computer science program that covers both hardware and software because in the field it is necessary to be familiar with both.

There are a number of different degree programs offered, and the exact titles of the degrees can vary. The most common areas of study are computer science and information technology. A degree program in these areas provides a student with a general knowledge of computer hardware and software that is applicable to a wide range of jobs in the computer field. Courses in this field focus on designing, developing, and maintaining computer systems. Students usually study computer networking, hardware and software, communication systems, mobile computing, Web applications, security, and the overall management of company-wide technology. It is also possible to study information systems technology, which includes using and maintaining databases. This is particularly useful for those interested in database administration.

TECHNICAL SKILLS

When students study computer science or information technology, they take a variety of different courses. They must take courses in mathematics and physics. Mathematics courses typically include advanced forms of calculus and algebra, as well as statistics and probability.

Students also take courses in several areas of computer science. General courses on the subject provide the basic knowledge necessary to understand and work with computers. Examples of such courses include introduction to computer systems, introduction to data structures, and computational mathematics.

Although computer support professionals are not computer programmers who write applications or original programs, they must still be familiar with the programming

A student makes an adjustment to a computerized "robot receptionist." Colleges often have staff engaged in research and offer students the opportunity to work with emerging technologies.

languages that are commonly used to communicate with computers. Therefore, computer science students, regardless of their special area of interest, take programming courses in specific languages such as C and Unix. Computer support personnel may work with computer systems or software applications that run on these languages, and they have to be able to issue commands to the computer in them.

Students can also take courses in the areas of the industry that interest them, such as automation or robotics. It is a good idea to take at least one basic computer engineering course, which explains in detail the principles of how computer hardware works. Computer systems design can also be a useful course to take. Many computer support professionals design networks of computer systems and peripherals, either for their own company or for a company's clients.

Some institutions offer special courses in communication and business for engineers and other techies. If such a course is available, taking it is highly recommended. Communicating technical information to nontechnical users and businesspeople is always an issue in computer support. In addition, it can be very helpful to be familiar with the business issues companies face. For example, those interested in database administration must be able to understand the kinds of data and reports that are important to the company.

Other courses may include ethical computing, which focuses on keeping data confidential and protecting people's privacy, and computer security, which focuses on protecting computer systems and data from unauthorized access. Maintaining the security of computer systems and data is of major importance in any computer support job today.

Students will most likely perform exercises in a computer lab as part of their college courses. Here, they will perform actual computer-related tasks and learn through hands-on experience.

Some students might want to prepare for a computer support job in a particular industry, such as energy systems, factory automation, telecommunications, or health care/medical technology. In this case, it is possible to combine training in computer science with courses in these fields. Having specific industry knowledge in addition to general computer hardware and software skills can make one a highly desirable job candidate for that particular industry.

Computer support and information technology do not exist in a vacuum. To be successful at running computer projects, a person must know how to manage people and projects in general. In most cases, computer support is more than fixing a computer. The further one goes in one's career, the larger the projects become and the more people are involved. Therefore, understanding project management is very important. Project management is the allocation of people and resources so that the necessary work gets done correctly, on time, and within budget. Learning project management software and taking courses in management can pay off once a person is in the real world, faced with running projects. In addition, it may be helpful to take a course in basic finance so that one is familiar with functions such as how to create a budget. Working in IT is like working in any other part of an organization— expenditures must be tracked and purchases justified. All of this knowledge will be helpful to someone hoping to advance in a career.

Perhaps most important, college is a time to develop good work habits. In computer support, employees are expected to work quickly, accurately, and with attention to detail, so that users can get back to their own work without further problems. Success in the field depends on one's ability to do this, so start now. Do your work on time in a thorough and correct way. Develop work habits that will advance your career once you are working in the real world.

NONTECHNICAL SKILLS

As in most undergraduate degree programs, students in computer science are usually required to take a variety of general courses in the humanities and arts. Students should take advantage of this opportunity. Because of the multicultural nature of the business and technical world today, it is useful to have knowledge that helps you understand other people and cultures. Working in the computer field, one will interact with coworkers, managers, and users from a wide range of cultural backgrounds. Also, today's businesses are global. Often people from a variety of different countries must work together. It's common today to work for a company that has branches in multiple countries and customers throughout the world. Computer support professionals may work with colleagues from other countries and may even have to travel internationally to work on projects. Even within the United States and Canada, there are different cultures in different parts of the country. Use your liberal arts courses to learn more about subjects such as history, psychology, languages, and literature, which will help

Many companies today have branches in multiple countries. Therefore, it is useful to take courses in college that will increase your understanding of people from different cultures.

you better understand the people you will meet in your job. Understanding other people's cultures and beliefs helps you interact with them, creates a positive impression, and makes work go more smoothly.

Having a broad range of knowledge allows you to demonstrate to potential employers that you can understand the company's business as well as its technology. Further, it shows that you can understand and work with other people, including customers, suppliers, and business partners. This is a highly valued skill in today's business world.

SCHOLARSHIPS AND GRANTS

Today more than ever, college can be expensive. There are a number of resources available to help students cover some of the costs of pursuing an education in computer science. The Institute of Electrical and Electronics Engineers (IEEE) has a special student Web site (http://www.ieeeusa.org/careers/student.menu.html) that contains links to information on scholarships, grants, and technical contests open to students attending college. The American Society for Engineering Education (ASEE) hosts a Web site (http://students.egfi-k12.org) for students in high school. Along with other information, it contains a list of organizations that provide scholarships for students interested in studying technology and engineering.

A number of U.S. government organizations also offer scholarships and tuition assistance programs to computer science students who are willing to work for the government after college. For example, the National Security Agency (NSA) offers the National Security Education Program (http://www.nsep.gov). For those who are interested in military service, many branches of the armed services offer ROTC programs that will pay for all or part of a college education in a technical field such as computer science. If you are interested in enlisting in the military, check out the educational reimbursement programs available before enrolling in college.

INTERNSHIPS

One challenge faced by students is how to get a job fresh out of school, when they have no experience. For employers, hiring a person who has no experience means taking a risk. In contrast, having hands-on experience demonstrates to employers that one can perform the tasks the job requires. So how do students gain experience without having a job?

One way to gain experience is to obtain an internship at a company. Internships are unpaid positions that provide students with the opportunity to learn skills on the job. Interns perform basic tasks, assisting professionals in the field. Through internships, students can gain hands-on experience working with computer hardware, software, and networks. Internships provide an invaluable opportunity to see how the tools and techniques learned in school are used on the job. They give students the chance to observe how computer support professionals deal with people and issues in the workplace and how projects are carried out in the real world. Internships provide another benefit as well: if a student does a good job as an intern, the employer will likely provide him or her with a reference letter to use with job applications. In addition, the intern's supervisors and coworkers may be able to help with job leads when the student starts looking for work.

College students can do internships during the summer or other school breaks, or work part-time at an internship during the academic year. Some colleges offer a cooperative learning program, which includes a semester or more of an internship or work placement in addition to academic studies. Other internships do not require enrollment in college; they require only a high school diploma and hands-on skills.

To look for internship opportunities, go to the job and career Web site of the Association for Computing Machinery (ACM) at http://jobs.acm.org and search for internships. The IEEE, another major technology and engineering society, provides information on internships through its student resources page (http://www.ieeeusa.org/careers /student.menu.html).

GAINING EXPERIENCE THROUGH VOLUNTEER WORK

Potential employers in the computer field are always looking for previous experience when they interview applicants. Another great way to gain experience is through volunteer work. This approach allows you to develop your technical and people skills, while helping others at the same time. While you are in high school or college, you can donate some of

Volunteering to teach others how to use computers provides students with hands-on experience. It also provides the satisfaction of helping others in the community.

your time and computer expertise to an organization such as the Boys & Girls Clubs of America, Boy Scouts of America, or Girl Scouts of the USA, helping young people learn to use computers. Or you might help a small nonprofit or charity in your area set up and maintain its computer systems.

You can also hone your skills by participating in forums on the Internet where users post problems they are having with their computers or software. Many manufacturers have an informal network of "experts" who help others solve problems with their products. These include Apple Geniuses and Microsoft MVPs. Helping users through online communities can help you gain experience dealing with users and solving problems. It also gives you a chance to observe how other computer professionals tackle problems.

On a more formal level, organizations such as the ACM and IEEE offer student memberships. If you are serious about a computer support career, joining and participating in the student activities of such organizations can provide you with real-world knowledge. It can also provide the opportunity to meet professionals who are working in the field. Professionals are often willing to assist students and may be able to offer advice on a project you need help with. Also, the contacts you make when participating in industry events may be able to help you with information on internships or employment leads when the time comes to look for a job. When you start working at your first job, these contacts may also be valuable sources of advice and information.

The ACM, in partnership with major software manufacturers, provides student versions of products to its student members. The ACM also offers a special newsletter for students. The IEEE offers a variety of programs especially for students.

CHAPTER 5

Finding Employment in Computer Support

The way in which job hunters locate positions has changed considerably over the past decade, especially in technical fields such as information technology. Often when people think about searching for a job, they first think of looking for advertised openings. There is nothing wrong with applying for a position one finds this way, but it is usually not the most effective way of obtaining a job. One problem with this approach is that every published ad gets an enormous number of responses, especially when the economy is stagnant and unemployment is high. Also, only a small number of all available jobs show up in ads. So, how does one find a computer support job?

Finding and landing a job in computer support requires planning, preparation, and persistence. The following sections explain how to locate a job in computer support. You'll learn how a candidate should present himself or herself, both on paper and in person, to potential employers and how to maximize the chances of obtaining a job. Finally, you'll learn what to expect once you land a job in computer support.

COLLEGE RESOURCES

For those who attend college or technical school, one resource worth checking out is the placement office. This facility is set

Students talk to company representatives at a college job fair. Attending job fairs allows students to learn about opportunities at major companies within and outside their local area.

up to assist students in finding jobs. The placement office helps students research and contact companies and provides assistance with résumé preparation. Another method of identifying potential employers is attending job fairs. These are events to which companies send representatives to talk to potential applicants. While some job fairs are held at colleges, others are held in communities and are open to the general public. Often companies are looking to fill technical positions, including computer support jobs. Job fairs provide an excellent opportunity to learn about specific companies. Since most companies today need computer professionals, it is worth asking about information technology positions at companies that interest you, even if they are not specifically advertised.

ONLINE WANT ADS

One of the most common ways to advertise for employees today is posting a want ad online. This practice has long been common among technology companies, and it has become increasingly routine for companies of all types. Computer companies and information technology departments in many organizations prefer to advertise for employees online for a number of reasons. It's cost-effective, the staff is comfortable using computer technology, and the responses come in faster, speeding up the hiring process. Also, respondents can demonstrate their familiarity with computer technology just by responding electronically.

Among the top job-posting sites are CareerBuilder.com and Monster.com. In addition, it is worth visiting the Web sites of individual companies and government agencies, many of which post job listings on their sites. This is a cost-effective way for companies to advertise for employees, so it has become very popular. When you respond to an online ad, you send a copy of your résumé electronically. Once the company has your résumé, the staff evaluates it just as they would a paper résumé.

NETWORKING

One of the best ways to find a job is by networking. Once a person is working in an industry, he or she has the opportunity

Networking is key to a successful job search. One effective method is to have friends or family give one's résumé to the technology manager at the company where they work.

to develop contacts with other professionals in the field. So when that person needs to look for another job, he or she can call acquaintances and colleagues to ask if they know of any jobs that are available.

How do people network, though, when looking for a first job? One way is to talk to family, friends, and the people they know. Find people who work at the kinds of companies that interest you. Ask them whom you should talk to about a computer job at their companies.

Another approach is to call or e-mail an IT manager or IT director at a company, tell that person you are a student, and ask for advice about getting a job in IT. Managers are frequently willing to help students learn more about their field, and they may be willing to grant you an informational interview. This type of interview is not focused on finding an immediate position. Instead, it helps you learn more about some of the opportunities available and the steps you need to take to get a first job in computer support. Getting your foot in the door to speak to key people in the field is very important. In addition to giving you useful advice that can shorten your search, they may personally know of contacts that are looking for employees.

Joining one of the electronics organizations such as the IEEE or ACM at the student level can be an advantage when it comes to networking and job hunting. Such organizations maintain job opening information on their Web sites. More important, participating in projects as a student member often involves contact with computer professionals. These people become contacts one can call on for help in finding a job later. Even if a student has not participated in a computer industry organization while in school, it's a good idea to join after graduating. Such organizations offer a range of job-hunting resources to their members, including newsletters with job openings and online job information.

It's a good idea to get the name, e-mail address, phone number, and, if possible, business card of anyone you meet in the computer field while you are in school. This allows you to contact that person later when looking for job leads. If someone you contact doesn't have any leads, you can ask if he or she can provide the names of other people who might be able to help.

CERTIFICATIONS FOR COMPUTER SUPPORT

Getting certified in particular computer technologies can make an applicant more attractive to potential employers, who want to make sure employees have the skills they need. Many companies offer certifications in their products and technologies. These certifications usually require one to study a particular technology in detail. Often this involves studying a book or manual about the technology and then taking and passing an online exam.

Manufacturers offer a variety of certifications for different computer professionals and technologies. For example, software manufacturer Microsoft offers a certification called Microsoft Certified Technology Specialist (MCTS). According to Microsoft, "MCTS candidates are capable of implementing, building, troubleshooting, and debugging a particular Microsoft technology." The MCTS is granted for mastery of a Microsoft technology such as the Windows operating system or the Microsoft SQL database. Those who achieve mastery of a variety of Microsoft technologies can qualify for a higher level of certification, Microsoft Certified IT Professional (MCITP). Hardware manufacturer Cisco Systems offers five levels of certification in areas such as network architecture and network security. The levels range from entry-level to career professional. These are only two examples of the many companies offering certification in their technologies.

RECRUITMENT AGENCIES

Recruitment agencies—sometimes referred to as headhunters—are hired by companies to find employees. Because qualified computer professionals are in high demand, recruiters are often looking for them. Job seekers can find recruitment agencies in a given geographic area in the phone book or online. Applicants can send each one a résumé and cover letter, just as with individual companies. Recruitment agencies can be a more valuable resource once an applicant has some experience in the field and is interested in moving to a higher-level job.

Professional and community organizations sometimes organize networking nights or job fairs. These events give job seekers a chance to meet and share their résumés with company representatives.

DISTRIBUTING RÉSUMÉS

Don't limit yourself to sending résumés only to companies that have print or online ads. Companies, especially large ones, have positions opening up all the time, and many are filled without being advertised. The trick to getting a job is to get a large number of résumés into the hands of potential employers. Sometimes the hiring manager has a job that has not yet been advertised. Other times the manager files the résumé away in case he or she needs to fill a job opening later. Going through a file of résumés is less expensive than paying for an ad. Sometimes the person who receives the résumé passes it on to someone else who is looking for a qualified person to fill a position.

How do you know which companies to send résumés to? You'll have to do a little bit of research. For example, you can use directories published by companies such as Standard & Poor's or Dunn & Bradstreet. These directories contain detailed information about a huge number of businesses. Copies of these directories are available at most libraries. You can also use printed or online directories of companies in a particular industry. Most industries have industry associations that publish such directories, listing their members. Your local librarian can help you find this information.

Once you have created a list of target companies, send your résumé to the director of information technology or human resources. It is best to use that person's name, rather than "Dear Sir or Madam." Search on the company's Web site or call the company's receptionist to find the correct name.

Include a brief cover letter explaining the type of job you are interested in, and briefly note why you think your education and experience would benefit the company. For some good examples, check out some of the many books available on writing résumés and cover letters.

It's important to remember that sending out résumés is only the start of the job-hunting process. The purpose of sending out résumés is to obtain a job interview. The key to getting job interviews is persistence. You may have to send out many résumés and keep sending out more every week until you get interviews and, eventually, a job.

TEMPORARY WORK

While you are looking for a permanent job, consider applying for a temporary job in computer support. There are temporary employment agencies that specialize in supplying computer service personnel to companies that have short-term projects or need someone to fill in for an employee who is temporarily unavailable.

There are several advantages to taking a temporary computer support job while looking for a full-time position. First, it provides a source of income while you search for a job. Second, it's not unusual for temporary employees to later be offered a permanent position if they perform well. Third, it provides you with job experience, which can then be added to your résumé. Finally, the professionals you meet in a temporary job might be able to provide a reference or refer you to other contacts who are looking for an employee.

RÉSUMÉ PREPARATION

In order to gain an interview with a prospective employer, it is necessary to present your background, education, and skills in a way that shows you are qualified for the position. The vehicle one uses to do this is the résumé. There are many formats that can be used for a résumé. However, in today's tough job market, employers often receive a large number of résumés in response to every ad they post. Those in charge of sorting through these résumés are unlikely to spend a lot of time searching for key information on any one résumé. Therefore, it is best to stick with a simple résumé format that makes it easy to tell what type of job you are seeking and what your past experience is. Clearly label sections of the résumé, using headings such as "Experience" and "Education." List all relevant paid or volunteer positions under "Experience," in reverse chronological order.

Before you send a résumé to a company in response to an ad, research the company and its industry. This is easy to do online. This research allows you to structure your résumé so that it emphasizes points that are relevant to the company and the specific job you are applying for. For instance, if you are applying to a computer services company, you could emphasize aspects of your experience and education that demonstrate how well you work with customers, solve problems, and meet deadlines.

Although technical skills are necessary to perform a computer support job, a potential employer will look for other skills as well. Computer support staff must be able to work well with customers and as part of a team. Therefore,

To maximize your chances for an interview, research companies online before sending your résumé. This allows you to tailor your résumé to the company's particular industry, activities, and needs.

you should highlight any nontechnical skills that would contribute to your success in the job. This might include organizational skills, such as planning events, organizing meetings, or preparing multimedia presentations. If you have taken courses in business areas, such as project management, budgeting, or finance, indicate that you have training in those areas.

Examples of work experience can include paid jobs, volunteer work, internships, and school activities. When describing your experience, don't just say what you did on the job— indicate the benefits of what you did. For example, you might write: "Upgraded computers in the computer lab so that students could access information more quickly, allowing more students to use the facility on a daily basis." Or: "Acquired used computers and set them up for inner-city youth program so that students could learn computer skills that would help them get jobs." By showing the benefits of your activities at work or as a volunteer, you demonstrate that you are the type of person who identifies needs and addresses them and who is interested in and capable of making a contribution to the organization.

There's no need to include a lot of information about your personal interests, unless they are relevant to the job. For instance, if you are applying to the IT department at a charity involved with animals, it would be relevant to mention that you've done volunteer work in pet rescue. Also, if you've donated your time to help a nonprofit organization with computer issues, mention this fact. Today many companies are interested in being good corporate citizens that contribute to the communities where they are located.

Possibly the most important step in preparing a résumé is making sure it is error-free. Thoroughly proofread your résumé, and have someone else do so as well. Don't rely on computer spell-checkers to find errors. They don't always catch errors such as missing words and incorrect words (such as "hole" instead of "whole"). Computer support is a field that requires attention to detail, and presenting a résumé that is sloppy, looks unprofessional, or contains errors can lead an employer to think that you will do slipshod work in the field.

THE INTERVIEW PROCESS

Once you are invited for an interview, you must convince the prospective employer that you are the best person for the job. The first thing an interviewer notices is the physical appearance of an applicant. So the first step in being successful in an interview is to appear professional. Wear business-appropriate clothing and be well groomed.

It is common in the computer field for candidates to be interviewed by numerous people. After meeting one-on-one with the IT manager, a candidate will often meet with other department employees. Managers want to make sure that all members of their team can work well together. In small companies, senior management may interview candidates as well. Candidates should treat everyone they meet respectfully and politely. Answer questions, even difficult ones, calmly, using correct grammar.

To maximize your chances of success in the interview, look up information on the company so that you can show you understand the organization's goals and what its computer support needs might be. When you are asked about how you

Candidates for computer support jobs will often interview with other department employees in addition to the IT manager, so the manager can get their input on the hiring decision.

would approach a problem, try to answer in a way that shows you understand the real-world concerns of a company like theirs. For instance, you might point out that a solution saves money or improves reliability.

Be prepared to answer difficult questions as well as straightforward ones. If you are asked about skills or experience you don't have, explain why your previous experience and education have equipped you to learn those skills. Interviewers will sometimes ask questions designed to test how candidates solve problems. Be aware that if an interviewer asks how you would handle a situation, he or she may not be looking for a particular solution. Instead, he or she may be in interested in seeing how you break a problem down and analyze it, or how you respond when faced with a difficult question on the spot. On the other hand, some questions, such as how you apply a particular technology, are designed to establish whether you are knowledgeable about that technology. Other questions, such as "What is your greatest weakness?," are designed to see how well you react when faced with an awkward or stressful situation.

One way to be prepared for difficult questions is to rehearse the answers to them before you start going to interviews. For example, "I'm sometimes impatient; I want to get things done right away" is an acceptable answer to the weakness question, since that "weakness" can be valuable in a fast-paced workplace. If you know how to respond before you are asked, you won't have to think of an answer when you are faced with the stress of the interview. When asked how you would handle a particular problem, a good approach is to explain how you handled a similar or related problem in the past. Finally, be sure to follow up after the interview by sending a thank-you note expressing your appreciation for the interview.

WORKING AS A COMPUTER SUPPORT PROFESSIONAL

The computer support professional's job is to keep an organization's computer systems working, maximizing the time they are available to users. This involves long-term tasks, such as upgrading software, monitoring performance, backing up data on the system, and installing security software. At the same time, during a typical day, computer support professionals will be faced with short-term tasks that need to be done. They might have to address user problems, such as a computer that is not working or a smartphone that needs to be set up to access the company's e-mail system. They might need to obtain approval for ordering additional hard drives for data storage, or set up an account for a new employee so that he or she can access the network.

Computer support professionals need to be very organized. They must be able to identify which tasks have the highest priority and arrange a schedule to get both long-term and short-term tasks done. They must also keep accurate, detailed records, for example, to keep track of the different versions of hardware and software used in the organization. They must schedule routine maintenance to keep hardware running and software up to date. Computer support professionals may be on call some days; often, people in an IT department will take turns on a daily or weekly basis. When on call, computer support staff may receive phone calls from users outside of normal working hours. They will try to walk users through the steps necessary to solve their computer problem. In some cases, they may have to go in to the office to solve a problem.

Computer support managers have managerial responsibilities. They must make and track budgets. They must evaluate what equipment is necessary to meet the company's future needs, get approval from senior management to purchase it, and then oversee the installation and testing of the new equipment. They must hire, supervise, review, and sometimes fire employees working for them.

KEEPING UP WITH THE FIELD

Nothing changes faster than computer technology. New versions of computer hardware and software are continually emerging, and entirely new technologies are constantly coming along. A few years ago, there were no tablet computers, no cell phones that could surf the Internet, and no cloud computing. Computer support is not a field in which a person can stop learning after graduation and still have a long career. Keeping up with the newest hardware, software, computer languages, and technologies is critical for computer support professionals. They must constantly glean information from books, courses, trade magazines, and other resources to learn how to use and maintain the latest technologies. Joining and participating in professional organizations in the field is another way to learn about new and developing technologies and perhaps play a role in their development. A career in computer support means a commitment to learning throughout one's career.

algorithm A series of steps that tell a computer how to perform a task.

application A computer program designed for a specific function or task.

bureaucracy A system involving many rules, procedures, and regulations and numerous levels of management.

cloud computing The practice of storing computer data on servers that can be accessed through the Internet rather than on one's own computer system.

cybersecurity Measures taken to protect a computer or computer system against unauthorized access or attack.

database A collection of computerized records, organized for rapid search and retrieval of information.

download To transfer data, such as a software file, to one's computer from a remote computer.

driver A software program that provides instructions to a computer about how to run a component or peripheral.

drone A remotely controlled unmanned vehicle.

freelance Providing services independently and on temporary contracts rather than as an employee.

independent contractor A person who works for himself or herself and is employed by others on an as-needed or contract basis rather than as a full-time employee.

information technology The branch of engineering that deals with the development, implementation, and maintenance of computer hardware and software systems to organize and communicate information.

intelligence In military and law enforcement organizations, information on threats, enemies, and other situations relevant to accomplishing missions.

intranet A local or restricted computer network, such as one within a company.

inventory The quantity of goods, parts, or products that a company has on hand.

maintenance The process of keeping something in good working order.

multimedia The use of computers to combine different types of media, such as text, graphics, video, and sound.

network A group of interconnected computer systems.

operating system The software that controls the basic functions of a computer.

overhead The expenses involved in running a business, such as rent and utilities.

patch A software update issued by a software manufacturer in between major revisions of the software in order to fix problems.

retail The sale of goods and services directly to consumers; the industry of such selling.

server A powerful computer that provides data and services to networked computers.

software-as-a-service (SaaS) A software distribution model in which applications are hosted and maintained by a service provider and made available to customers over the Internet for a subscription fee.

troubleshooting The act of identifying and fixing malfunctions in a computer system.

American Society for Engineering Education (ASEE)
1818 N Street NW, Suite 600
Washington, DC 20036-2479
(202) 331-3500
Web site: http://www.asee.org
The ASEE is a nonprofit organization of individuals and
institutions committed to furthering education in engineering and engineering technology. The organization
provides technology education and career resources for
students grades K–12, including a student newsletter,
magazine, blog, and career center.

Association for Computing Machinery (ACM)
2 Penn Plaza, Suite 701
New York, NY 10121-0701
(800) 342-6626
Web site: http://www.acm.org
This educational and scientific computing society deliv-
ers resources that advance computing as a science and
profession. The organization maintains a career center
and offers online books and courses for members. It also
has special interest groups that focus on specific areas of
computer science. ACM accepts student members.

Computer History Museum
1401 N. Shoreline Boulevard
Mountain View, CA 94043
(650) 810-1010

Web site: http://www.computerhistory.org

The mission of the Computer History Museum is to preserve and present for posterity the artifacts and stories of the information age. In addition to providing a variety of exhibits on-site, the museum maintains an illustrated history of the computer online.

Computing Technology Industry Association (CompTIA)
3500 Lacey Road, Suite 100
Downers Grove, IL 60515
(630) 678-8300

Web site: http://www.comptia.org

CompTIA is a nonprofit trade association that serves as the voice of the world's information technology (IT) industry. The organization focuses its programs on four main areas: education, certification, advocacy, and philanthropy. Its Web site offers information on a variety of career paths within IT.

IEEE—Student Branch
1828 L Street NW, Suite 1202
Washington, DC 20036-5104
(800) 678-4333

Web site: http://www.ieee.org/web/membership/students/index1.html

Formerly known as the Institute of Electrical and Electronics Engineers, IEEE provides education and career resources for the use of students in computer and technology fields.

Information Technology Association of Canada (ITAC)
5090 Explorer Drive, Suite 801

Mississauga, ON L4W 4T9

Canada

(905) 602-8345

Web site: http://www.itac.ca

This organization sponsors a variety of forums on IT topics, publishes research reports on various aspects of the IT industry in Canada, and provides the latest news on its Web site.

Software & Information Industry Association (SIIA)

1090 Vermont Avenue NW, Sixth Floor

Washington, DC 20005-4095

(202) 289-7442

Web site: http://www.siia.net

This organization offers a variety of daily and weekly news-letters on the software industry as well as informational meetings and Webcasts.

WEB SITES

Due to the changing nature of Internet links, Rosen Publishing has developed an online list of Web sites related to the subject of this book. This site is updated regularly. Please use this link to access the list:

http://www.rosenlinks.com/CICT/Supp

For Further Reading

Bolles, Richard Nelson. *What Color Is Your Parachute? A Practical Manual for Job-Hunters and Career-Changers.* 40th anniversary ed. Berkeley, CA: Ten Speed Press, 2012.

Crompton, Diane, and Ellen Sautter. *Finding a Job Through Social Networking: Use LinkedIn, Twitter, Facebook, Blogs, and More to Advance Your Career.* 2nd ed. Indianapolis, IN: JIST Works, 2011.

Enelow, Wendy, and Louise Kursmark. *Expert Resumes for Computer and Web Jobs.* 3rd ed. Indianapolis, IN: JIST Publishing, 2011.

Farr, Michael. *Top 100 Computer and Technical Careers: Your Complete Guidebook to Major Jobs in Many Fields at All Training Levels.* 4th ed. Indianapolis, IN: JIST Publishing, 2009.

Ferguson Publishing. *Computers* (Discovering Careers). New York, NY: Ferguson's, 2011.

Field, Shelly. *Ferguson Career Coach: Managing Your Career in the Computer Industry.* New York, NY: Ferguson, 2009.

Gookin, Dan. *Troubleshooting and Maintaining Your PC All-in-One for Dummies.* Hoboken, NJ: John Wiley and Sons, 2011.

Info Tech Employment. *Information Technology Jobs in America 2012: Corporate & Government Career Guide: Why You Want One, Where They Are, How to Get One.* New York, NY: Info Tech Employment, 2012.

Kirk, Amanda. *Information Technology* (Field Guides to Finding a New Career). New York, NY: Ferguson, 2009.

Kraynak, Joe. *The Complete Idiot's Guide to PC Basics: Windows 7 Edition*. Indianapolis, IN: Alpha, 2011.

McGraw-Hill. *Resumes for Computer Careers*. 3rd ed. New York, NY: McGraw-Hill, 2008.

Miller, Michael. *Absolute Beginner's Guide to Computer Science*. New York, NY: Que Publishing/Pearson Technology, 2009.

Morley, Deborah, and Charles S. Parker. *Understanding Computers: Today and Tomorrow*. 14th ed. Boston, MA: Course Technology Cengage Learning, 2013.

WetFeet. *Careers in Information Technology* (Insider Guide). Philadelphia, PA: WetFeet, 2009.

Bibliography

American Society for Engineering Education
    (ASEE). "High School: Science and Engineering
    Fellowship Program." 2012. Retrieved August 27,
    2012 (http://www.asee.org/fellowship-programs
    /high-school).

American Society for Engineering Education (ASEE).
    "Undergraduate." 2012. Retrieved August 27, 2012
    (http://www.asee.org/fellowship-programs
    /undergraduate).

Brookshear, J. Glenn. *Computer Science: An Overview.* 11th ed.
    Boston, MA: Addison-Wesley, 2011.

Byers, Peg. "Day in the Life of an IT Professional—Database
    Administrator." Course Technology/Cengage Learning,
    2012. Retrieved September 2, 2012 (http://www.course
    .com/careers/dayinthelife/dba_jobdesc.cfm).

Cisco. "IT Certification and Career Paths." 2012. Retrieved
    September 15, 2012 (http://www.cisco.com/web
    /learning/le3/learning_career_certifications_and
    _learning_paths_home.html).

Freedman, Miles. Interview with author. September 15, 2012.

Institute of Electrical and Electronics Engineers (IEEE).
    "IEEE Student Job Site for Entry Level Jobs."
    AfterCollege.com, 2012. Retrieved August 26, 2012
    (http://www.aftercollege.com/career-networks
    /aftercollege/ieee-entry-level-jobs).

Institute of Electrical and Electronics Engineers (IEEE).
    "Student Awards, Scholarships, and Fellowships." 2012.

Retrieved August 26, 2012 (http://www.ieee.org
/membership_services/membership/students/awards
/sag.html).

Marcus, Miriam. "The Best Way to Find (and Fill) a Job
Online." Forbes.com, May 26, 2009. Retrieved September
20, 2012 (http://www.forbes.com/2009/05/26/job
-seeking-websites-entrepreneurs-human-resources
-monster.html).

McDowell, Gayle Laakmann. *The Google Resume: How to
Prepare for a Career and Land a Job at Apple, Microsoft, Google,
or Any Top Tech Company.* Hoboken, NJ: Wiley, 2011.

Microsoft. "Microsoft Certifications Path and FAQ—
Microsoft Learning." 2012. Retrieved September 20, 2012
(http://www.microsoft.com/learning/en/us
/certification/cert-overview.aspx).

National Security Agency (NSA)/Central Security Service
(CSS). "Cyber Careers and More at the National Security
Agency (NSA)." 2012. Retrieved July 26, 2012 (http://
www.nsa.gov/careers/index.shtml).

The Princeton Review. "Systems Administrator."
2012. Retrieved September 3, 2012 (http://www
.princetonreview.com/Careers.aspx?cid=209).

Topi, Heikki, et al. "IS 2010 Curriculum Guidelines for
Undergraduate Degree Programs in Information
Systems." Association for Computing Machinery (ACM)
and Association for Information Systems (AIS), 2010.
Retrieved August 27, 2012 (http://www.acm.org
/education/curricula/IS%202010%20ACM%20final.pdf).

U.S. Bureau of Labor Statistics (BLS). "Computer Support
Specialists—Occupational Outlook Handbook."

Retrieved September 1, 2012 (http://www.bls.gov/ooh
/computer-and-information-technology/computer
-support-specialists.htm).

Watson, Joe. *Where the Jobs Are Now: The Fastest-Growing
Industries and How to Break Into Them.* New York, NY:
McGraw-Hill, 2010.

Woodall, Tony. "Day in the Life of an IT Professional—
Network Administrator." Course Technology/Cengage
Learning, 2012. Retrieved September 2, 2012 (http://
www.course.com/careers/dayinthelife/networkadmin
_jobdesc.cfm).

ABOUT THE AUTHOR

Jeri Freedman has a B.A. degree from Harvard University. For fifteen years she worked for high-technology companies involved in cutting-edge technologies, including advanced semiconductors and scientific testing equipment. She is the author of numerous young adult nonfiction books, including *Digital Career Building Through Skinning and Modding* and *Online Safety*.

PHOTO CREDITS

Cover (front inset) © iStockphoto.com/Baran Özdemir; cover (background), p. 1 © iStockphoto.com/Andrey Prokhorov; pp. 5, 13, 18, 45 Bloomberg/Getty Images; p. 7 © iStockphoto.com/Catherine Yeulet; p. 10 Baltimore Sun/McClatchy-Tribune/Getty Images; p. 11 Chip Somodevilla/Getty Images; p. 24 Wavebreak Media/Thinkstock; pp. 26, 35, 38, 41 © AP Images; p. 27 Comstock/Thinkstock; p. 29 Boston Globe/Getty Images; p. 48 Ableimages/Photodisc/Thinkstock; pp. 51, 56 John Moore/Getty Images; p. 53 Jack Hollingsworth/Photodisc/Thinkstock; p. 60 iStockphoto/Thinkstock; p. 63 Digital Vision/Thinkstock; interior pages border image © iStockphoto.com/Daniel Brunner; pp. 9, 19, 30–31, 46, 55 (text box background) © iStockphoto.com/Nicholas Belton.

Designer: Nicole Russo; Editor: Andrea Sclarow Paskoff; Photo Researcher: Amy Feinberg